WHERE THE WATERS
TAKE YOU

Where the Waters Take You

Poems by
Neil Harrison

PINYON PUBLISHING
Montrose, Colorado

ALSO BY
NEIL HARRISON

Story (chapbook)
In a River of Wind
Into the River Canyon at Dusk
Back in the Animal Kingdom

Cover Photograph "The Long Act of Falling" by Neil Harrison

Photograph of Neil Harrison by Kathleen Donnelly

Design by Susan Entsminger

First Edition: May 2018

Pinyon Publishing
23847 V66 Trail, Montrose, CO 81403
www.pinyon-publishing.com

Library of Congress Control Number: 2018940063
ISBN: 978-1-936671-50-2

for Kathleen

CONTENTS

THE LOST CHILD

An Evolution of History

WHERE THE WATERS TAKE YOU

The Lost Child

The Lost Child

There was a child, a boy or a girl,
no one now remembers, but
this child was always busy building
with whatever came to hand,
grass, dirt, dung, water, making
what no one else could imagine,
an entity of perpetual change,
without apparent beginning or end.

And absorbed in his or her unique vision,
the child was eventually lost to the world,
space and time both finally fading,
leaving that precocious creator alone,
still forming and forever adapting
this eternally unfinished home.

The Jungle

As a child, at times he'd kneel
in the backyard grass and watch
ants bustle in and out of their hills,
gathering the staples for survival
in their familiar reach of jungle.

And then he'd look up to consider
the scope of the world and find
the incomprehensible easy to accept—
time and space and the grand enigma
of myriad life-forms therein.

Caught up now in the cyber-hustle
with a wealth of technological playthings,
it's become more difficult to acknowledge
the limits of human perspective
and the very real probability that life
as we've come to know it is illusion.

These nights, when he steps outside
and stares up at those far lights
all but lost in black space, he ponders
our contemporary theories,
amounting, as they almost certainly do,
to little more than anthills in the jungle.

Already There

I think we all knew he was going somewhere,
the way he'd take off on his tricycle,
though it's clear now he was already there.

On that big red-and-white trike he'd tear
down the sidewalk as fast as he could pedal,
and we knew one day he was going somewhere

when he'd stop at the end of the block and stare
out beyond the field where we played ball.
It's clear now he was already there,

a world away from this Nebraska town, where
he could be himself and be acceptable.
And we all knew he was going somewhere,

just not how far he'd have to go to share
those instincts he was cursed or blessed to feel.
It's clear now he was already there,

on his roundabout way to New Orleans, where
he lived for a time, then faced death so well
we all still believed he was going somewhere.
Though it's clear now he was already there.

This Bike Path Now Called
The Cowboy Trail

Years ago it was the Cowboy Line,
a Chicago and Northwestern Railway branch
angling north and west out of Fremont
to the depot and switchyard here in Norfolk,
through the great roundhouse and on to O'Neill,
Valentine, Chadron, then into Wyoming.

Station helper in Spencer at fifteen,
Dad stuck with the railroad for forty-three years,
less two for the Great War and convalescence
from the mustard gas that killed his best friend.
Plainview, Neligh, Winnetoon, Bassett, and on
to Fremont, clerk, cashier, then agent in Norfolk
where he died of a stroke in '58.

Late in her life, Mom told us how she rode the train
out to Valentine to see her sister, pregnant
at the ranch southwest of Crookston,
how later, on his way out to pick her up,
Dad made it only as far as Long Pine
before his train bogged down, unable to buck
those towering winter-of-'49 drifts.

When I was twelve and my brother fourteen,
we walked west along those tracks,
each hunting a right-of-way,
flushing and missing bird after bird,
cursing, laughing, devil-may-care,
unaware at the time of those stories rooted
in that long pair of rails between us.

Handful of Pieces to a Puzzle Long Gone

The music of early dreams—
a drumming hammer,
sighing saw.

Raw scent of damp greenheads,
blood clotting serrated bills,
long gun leaning in a corner.

That sudden collapse
into confusion—
siren, lights, tears.

A flag-draped coffin.
lonely bugle,
seven rifles—

BYE.
    BYE.
        BYE.

The enormous
sense of silence
after a symphony.

Gardening

Again, tendrils of your climbing roses
anchor in the seam between roof and siding
on the south side of the garage, red blossoms
once more descending from the gutter to the ground.
A long rope of beautiful flowers, but chock-full of thorns
sure to shed blood when I trim the dying shoots.

Each spring I think of you, so patient with your gardens,
how you turned, raked and fertilized the ground,
seeded, weeded and watered, growing food for your family.
No doubt the duration made children more difficult,
the long years waiting for them to flower,
to establish for certain what had been planted,
and what might then be expected to grow.

When I quit a post-office-clerk position,
started school again and began to write,
you thought I'd thrown away all hope for a future,
along with good pay and a government pension.
But they couldn't pay enough to keep me sorting mail
through the long night, six nights a week, automaton
with a far bleaker future than at any of my prior
places of employment, including three years in the infantry.

Still, part of me understood your concern—teenager
during the Great Depression, you believed in practical things,
like hanging onto a good job, planting a garden
and growing your own food. Yet you fostered
these climbing roses, of no more obvious utility
than the words I'm planting here, weeding, watering,
always hoping something not-quite-practical flowers.

Thanksgiving

Once more obligated to be thankful,
families gather, and men stand by
as women bustle from the kitchen
to the dining room and back again.
Kids run in and out, upstairs and down,
yelling, laughing, now and then crying,
until dinner's ready and it's time at last
to give thanks, eat, compliment the cooks.

Eventually, enough is enough, and men
head for sofas, recliners, and proceed
to nod off while still pretending to watch
some game no one gives a damn about,
Women take care of leftovers, dishes,
catching up on the family news.
The bolder kids sneak drinks downstairs,
soon feeling warmed up well enough
to play doctor out in the garage.

This gathering of strangers, annually
struggling to shrug off discord and act
as if they belong, as though they ever did.
Until someone says, *It's time we got back*,
and once more everyone prepares to part,
each with a dawning sense of loss,
suddenly aware of having spent one more
year that will never come again.

Save Your Breath (for the dance)

Family often told my brother-in-law
smoking like he did would kill him.
Good advice, but it soured fast—
the more they preached, the more he smoked
to make it clear to one and all
it was his life and he'd live it his way.
And he did, by god, and it killed him.
But everybody's got to die somehow.

When it was her time to go,
Mom told me to look after my diabetic brother,
who'd made it clear he didn't want any help,
though while she lived she kept on trying.
And I told her I would, and I did I guess,
those times I could, when his blood sugar fell
so low he no longer recognized
who was trying to hand him the fix.

And maybe it was that childhood warning—
never take candy from a stranger—
but at times he'd try to swing at me,
and I'd hold his arms down and we'd stumble around
to the wild music of our barking dogs,
confused by the scene—him cursing, me laughing,
leading my brother in a drunken dance
while a Snickers bar, his favorite, did its slow work.

10

Olga

Grandma's youngest sister,
eighty six—too old, they said;
you might fall and break a hip.
But you wanted to fish again.

And I recalled those summers in the boat
out at the Refuge and up in Dakota,
you always talking Ernie
into hauling us kids along.

One afternoon, telling no one,
I took you out to the Loup canal,
set up lawn chairs, baited worms,
and we fished together in the cottonwood shade.

We caught nothing all day,
but you didn't fall,
just told old stories
and we laughed a lot.

And I summon that afternoon each time
I remember you bedridden
in the nursing home, crying,
All I want to do is die.

Cat-Skinner

Following the dogs this Sunday noon
past Cats and cranes along the hike-n-bike trail,
closed after flooding took out half a dozen bridges
and cut a fair chunk out of the path ahead,
I recall something my uncle told me forty years ago—

I don't know who's doin' their engineerin'
but that's the damdest idea I ever heard,
straightenin' the river so it won't wash out
so much ground from those farms upstream.

All they're doin's speedin' it up.
You get a goddamn big flood now
and when it hits these bends down here
it's gonna tear hell outta everything.

Cat jockey the better part of his life,
Wayne pushed dirt for ditches and dams
on irrigation projects throughout the Midwest,
and he didn't live to see that flood, but
he knew damned well what he was talking about.

All the Way

On summer mornings, blackbirds, robins
and rabbits scatter as the Happy dog bounds
out the back door and into the yard
to secure her familiar perimeter.
Back inside, after a hearty breakfast,
she's up on the couch, rooting and scooting
the throw pillows onto the floor before
she curls up and gives a great sigh of relief.
Six years old, she remains the pup
I know she will be till the end.
Smoke and the Gypsy both played and hunted,
excited as pups at seventeen,
each still conjuring the spirit of youth
all the too-short way to her grave.

Spring Burial in the Sandhills

After the service, the slow procession,
a multi-hued line of pickups and cars,
mini-vans and SUVs trailing west
from the church, then south into the hills.

At the gravesite the pastor's words
sweep east on the April wind,
and the faint trilling of cranes drifts down.

A carnival helix of the great wild birds
spirals upward far to the west,
winged escort singing you
up from the season of planting and birth,

out of the cyclic skein of time, where
what we here consign to the earth
has already flowered.

Paper Boats

—Ashes to ashes
Dr. Bob Johnson, 1920-2011

We put your remains into hand-made vessels,
one fashioned from a cardboard 12-pack,
the others from butcher paper, waxed side out,
hoping they'd float, for a time at least,
when Terry took them out in a kayak,
lit each afire and set it gently
adrift on the flooding Missouri,
where the flames engulfed them one by one,

and left you riding that current
you'd boated and fished for years,
on the river you lived and dreamed,
all of us gathered once more around you,
fulfilling your final request—this
last gesture of love, letting you go.

The Relative Dimensions of Memory

—remembering Larry Holland

Two days after Reese said, "Put this up,"
eleven years after your sudden death,
I'm staring at a color photograph
I took nearly twenty years ago.
In a red-checked shirt, hat, and faded jeans,
you smile past your pipe and a small wood fire,
a thin stand of lodgepole pines at your back,
the entire Bridger Wilderness beyond.

And all at once I'm viewing it through the lens,
focusing that camera I packed each time
we hiked back into the Wind River Range,
the dimensions dissolving until I'm both
with you there in the high country and
alone down here in the living room.

A Requiem ...

The air for you was such a generous house.
"A Requiem for a Teacher"
—Don Welch, 1932-2016

It's early, and warm this August morning
when the news comes and I step outside,

my thoughts on a teacher who raced pigeons,
a poet who wrote often of winged things.

Half a block west, the rumble of Harleys
heading north toward the rally in Sturgis

interrupts for a moment the summer
song of cicadas flexing their tymbals,

free at last of those brittle shells
clinging to the neighborhood trees,

cramped carapaces that finally cracked
after long interment and the night climb

to that high place of emergence where
the long-familiar dream of wings unfurled.

A Walk Along the River

February, late afternoon, fifty degrees,
a perfect time to take the dog out
for a walk at the wildlife management area,
where runoff had flooded the access trail,
so I parked on high ground near the road,
crossed the running water in a narrow place
and headed north, my wire-haired pointer
working parallel to me through a stand of trees,
where a crippled doe broke from the brush.

The dog took chase, and I yelled "No!"
but one, then the other, went over the bank,
and before I could tear through the brambles between us
they were halfway across the river.
I yelled again, though it was useless,
the dog I'd brought for a walk was gone,
lost somewhere way back in time,
as a wild predator now locked on prey
somewhere near three times her size,
barking, snapping, lunging for the neck
of the doe as she slashed out with sharp front hooves,
trying to knock the dog away or push her under,
both of them slipping away with the current
toward fallen trees piled in the bend ahead.

Running the bank as they rode the river,
I tried to keep close enough to reach the dog
if she swept into one of the snags and went under,
but they were in the channel and I was losing ground,
the current straight now, picking up speed,
while I ran into mud, falling farther behind,
and as they drifted into the next wide bend,
I slogged through a shallow backwater,
crossed a half-submerged beaver dam
and climbed the eight-foot riverbank
into another thicket, where they went out of sight.

When I saw them again, the doe was in the shallows,
the dog farther on, caught in the current,
trying to swim upstream, but drifting
slowly away from the now-stationary deer
toward a long downfall in the water.
"Here!" I yelled as I stumbled from the brush,
signaling for her to turn toward the bank,
and at last she swung around and paddled
just short of the deadfall into shallow water.

I watched the doe standing motionless
in ripples over a submerged sandbar,
until I got close enough to grab the dog
by the scruff and pull her away from the water,
out of sight of the deer so she wouldn't start again.
Through the thicket, down the high bank,
I crossed the beaver dam again, then stopped,
the dog no longer showing any interest.

I studied the deer still standing in the water
and knew the odds were she wouldn't make it out.
They'd battled for nearly a mile on the river,
each trying to put the other down,
and the doe clearly crippled from the start.
I waited, watching, hoping she'd move,
though each time she tried, she seemed off-balance.
At the time I thought she was just too weak,
but looking back I wonder if she'd stood too long,
sinking slowly in that loose, wet sand until
with just three good legs she couldn't pull herself out.

Beyond her the water was still blue as sky,
but shadows darkened the ripples where she stood,
the colors sharp now in the approaching dusk.
On the bank above her, young cottonwoods
stretched bone-white against the woods beyond.
And farther north, little mounds of snow
hung on beneath the cedars on the cemetery hill.
I turned and walked the dog out to the car.

My Brother's Place

He's still there, but the house is gone,
and the shed still standing where we tore it down
so he could put up a new metal building
some months before he died. The fencing
runs wrong too—where a string of steel posts stood
bordering the pasture to the east
a few half-buried lengths of wood
jut like tooth fragments long-diseased.
And too far south, the boundary line
takes a sudden drop into a deep ravine
where there's a water tank I almost recall,
though by now I know that's impossible.
This place, that tank and strange ravine—
none of it exists outside this dream.

An Evolution of History

An Evolution of History

What feral synapse in the age of stone
wedded the latent desire to the means
of beginning the tragic and triumphant
record of human endeavor?

Genesis an animated utterance
or some odd scratching in a pit of ash.
Apocalypse the final revelation,
Fire thou art, and unto fire shalt thou return.

In time, the epic becomes its own idol—
self-proclaimed shepherds gather meek sheep
as the merely myopic harken to the blind,
lords of war rise, princes of peace.

And through it all the hermits of god
commit themselves to adoration,
while the irreverent curse and carry on,
god-damning everything around them.

And all of it alive in each of us,
everywhere and always here, now.

At an Extraterrestrial Museum
in the Future

Now somewhere here we have …
the beginning and end of the Corporate Age,
one of the more inexplicable wonders
associated with this backwaters planetoid,

the whole of it represented …
if I can find it now … by an insubstantial
yet highly toxic layer of fossils
located, uh … right about …

here I would guess …
such an infinitesimal blip
it's nearly impossible to find
on the evolutionary ladder.

It appears that fear of falling
left them very near the bottom,
still desperately fastened
to the weakest rung at hand.

Their dogged refusal to let go
of outdated and inefficient sources of energy
at last rendered their planet entirely toxic—
i.e. they willfully exterminated themselves.

That Spring

Awakening to robin songs at dawn,
the sweet scent of apples on the breeze,
we met in our shared neighbor's lawn,
each chasing black-winged butterflies,
hoping they'd settle there, but they flew on,
across the alley to those flowering trees
we'd both been warned to leave alone,
where you began climbing, all elbows, knees,
those thighs I suddenly focused on,
until you met my gaze, and ill-at-ease,
into an altered world you stepped down,
the forbidden gate opened to our keys,
and innocence faded as we fell upon
the dying blossoms of the apple trees.

Dawn

—*Nu assoupi*, Balthus, 1980

On a cot near an angular table
with a pastel vase and flowers,
she leans on a checkered cushion
propped against a blue block wall,
nude but for socks, slippers, a white cloth
circling her brow like a crown,
head pillowed on a towel on the sill,
shutters open to the morning light.

Her eyes closed as though in sleep,
this portrait of prepubescent girlhood
would seem the picture of innocence
but for the artist's unseen presence,
her pale arms shielding her belly,
the rich color flaming at her cheek.

Photo of a Girl in the Great Depression

Raw adolescence in a canvas frame,
she stands before a makeshift shelter,
staring the cameraman down through his lens,
a grown man's hand-me-down undershirt
hanging like a filthy toga
from thin but undefeated shoulders.
Wild strands of matted black hair,
a scraped nose and swollen lip
paint her fresh from a recent fight,
while those dark eyes, still ablaze with threat,
acknowledge to everyone in sight
that she now stands fully prepared
to wrestle them into the common dirt
and tell the whole damned world her story.

An Answer for Everything

On camera, on the radio, I've heard them
ranting and raving about an economy
they long ago soared far above,
a war they have no personal stake in,
a religion founded on humble love
they've somehow warped into a means
to damn us all in that private hell
they preach, full of arrogance and hate.

These loud-mouthed, self-appointed pundits
with an answer for everything, nothing ever
out of reach of their egocentric ramblings
on this precarious planet, where
no one is guaranteed a next breath,
another of those countless unearned gifts
pulsing forth from the mystery
that both surrounds and fills us.

Addiction

Nothing quite so human as this
quest to get higher than ordinary
on whatever wings come to hand—
food, drink, sex, drugs, some
elusive degree of wealth or fame.

Gambling on those hollow feathers
fastened with that ancient glue, the dream,
another hero almost touching the sun
begins to awaken, already engaged
in the all too common fall.

Rapture

The second Tuesday of each month
the city's civil defense sirens
sound the voice of impending doom,
and my Drahthaar rockets off the couch,
tips her bearded muzzle to the heavens
and joins the neighborhood pack,
each ecstatic member rattling
another link in Darwin's chain.

One dozen sacred days each year
when that wailing starts all over town
and those canine trumpets answer,
the hair on the back of my neck comes up
as the fragile walls of time come down
all the way back to the genesis.

The Endless Scents of Memory

Driving past the dairy west of Wayne,
suddenly I'm back on the Verdigris
with Nick, my father's friend explaining
some of what he knows of outdoors lore,
much of it dated, like the term *shitepoke*
for what will become the great blue heron.
We listen to bullfrogs and meadowlarks
singing the praises of the spring-fed creek
as it winds itself through the prairie hills
and down around the legs of a dozen cows
knee-deep in fertile mud, cloaked in flies
and that indelible smell that will one day
carry Nick, that creek, and a boy like me
seventy miles and fifty years away.

After the Christmas Eve Service

The Christmas Eve after his death,
my German grandfather's extended family
gathered once more around the living room table
in his home a block north of the Lutheran church
where he'd served long years as an elder.

And in a rare appearance, an outlaw uncle
ducked in the back with a bottle of Seagram's
and sat drinking alone in the kitchen, until
an underage nephew slipped away to share
a shot for the shhweet baby Jesus.

Trouble Brewing

A watched pot never boils, they say,
but I'm standing in front of my microwave
at six o'clock this Tuesday morning,
watching my dollar-store carafe go around
like it's something interesting on TV.

I'm making some get-n-go coffee,
or at least I'm trying to with this
temperamental Walmart microwave
I bought for sixty-nine-ninety-five
on sale a couple of days ago.

I tried this same thing yesterday
and boiled coffee all *over* the place,
not enough left in the pot at the beep
for half a cup, and half of that was grounds.
You've *got* to keep an eye on it.

And that's what I'm doing this morning,
just waiting for it to screw up again
and leave me nothing but soggy grounds—
fair grounds for divorce in my book,
if I was married to it, *which* I ain't.

So it better do better this morning
or it'll find itself like a certain TV,
dead and buried a few years back,
every channel sporting some politician
spouting something I didn't care to hear.

All I gotta say to this Wally-World wonder is,
Do you feel lucky? Well, do you? Perk?
'Cuz I don't claim to be entirely sane
before a first dose of coffee in the morning.

Talking Shop

As students back in Norfolk High
we'd skip classes and head for the Elkhorn
when we needed a break, my friend and I,
then hunt or fish depending on the season.

One afternoon an odd piece of wood
atop a sandbar caught my attention,
and I picked it up, wondering aloud
what a guy might do with such a specimen.

"Make a helluva lamp," ventured Jake,
because that semester he was in shop class
and that's what they were supposed to make
for their final project if they wanted to pass.

After that, around every fire when we'd camp,
some piece of wood'd *make a helluva lamp*.

Ode to an Outhouse

That old adventure in being human
used to grace my uncle's Sandhills ranch,
though now and then it'd change location
so visitors had to either ask or search,
but if the wind was right it didn't take long
to pick up and follow that unique stench
back to where it hung eye-watering strong
at the source, two well-worn holes in a bench.
It was a study in non-discrimination,
an either-sex, dual-purpose reading room,
oftentimes a welcome destination
for the weary, warm and dark as a womb,
a place you left with a new sense of worth,
just another critter on the earth.

Too Wet to Work

I wake to steps on the front porch,
dress as they laugh in the kitchen.
Cigarette smoke and perking coffee
drown the scent of last night's rain.

Fishing the swollen river at dawn,
swarms of mosquitoes in the dripping brush,
my uncle strings a length of chicken gut
onto his line for bait and says,

After a rain like that last night,
them big cats bite like sons-a-bitches.

Lawn-Care with Babe

The neighbor's name was Harold
but folks called him "Babe" because
I was already over five feet tall
and neither he nor Clara was.

After long days at the sale barn,
like most of that dusty crew,
he'd head for Jake's to wait for the wife
and have a drink or two.

Summer days after work you'd find him
lying with his tools in the yard,
one hand tipping an Old Milwaukee,
the other brandishing a dandelion prod.

He'd cut strategic holes in his shoes
to ease a bad case of gout,
and when he asked if I'd help mow his yard
I agreed to help him out.

I was underage, but Babe liked his beer,
so every time I'd mow
he'd bring out a couple of Old Milwaukees,
and what kid's gonna say "no."

Late that summer his doctor told him
it was time to draw the line,
he'd have to quit the beer, but if he needed
he could have a small glass of wine.

Next time I mowed, Babe apologized,
"I can't offer a beer this time.
Doc shut me off," he said, then added,
"But I got some real good wine."

He led the way inside and didn't bother
to ask if I wanted any,
just poured us each an 8-ounce glass
of Mad-Dog 20/20.

Uncle Don

Forty-something and ankle-deep
in coarse Platte River gravel,
he plows upstream in search of a hole
deep enough to harbor fish.

My brother-in-law and I follow
his shirtless uncle upriver,
that pale skin a simmering
beacon in the July sun.

In boxer shorts and western boots
he kneels in a pool below a beaver den,
says, "Grab my feet," and ducks under,
clawing half out of sight beneath the bank.

We each grab a boot,
and when he gives a kick,
haul back hard and up he pops,
a two-pound carp in either hand.

"Git these …
on a stringer," he gasps,
"… there's more," and
down he goes again.

We grip his Acmes,
await another jerk,
then fish him out a second time,
a five-pound catfish clamped to his thumb.

"Fire up …
the grill," he sputters,
"… we're eatin' …
fish tonight."

The Happy Dog Horks Down
a Whole Damn Chicken

Each year my friend Ken heads up
to the Hutterite colony in South Dakota
to buy dressed chickens for himself and others,
and he calls me up last June and asks
if I want some, and I say "Sure, I'll take five
for myself and a couple for friends."

So with seven chickens on the way
I go downstairs to check the freezer
and damn!—I've still got three from last year
I must've forgot about, so I take one out,
head back upstairs, and put it in the sink to thaw
while I go to the store for barbecue sauce.

And I'm gone twenty minutes at most,
but when I get back there's nothing in the sink,
so I look around, and sure enough—
there's the plastic wrap the Hutterites use
and one thumbnail-sized bit of bone
on a chicken-sized wet spot on the couch
and that's all that's left of a 4-pound bird!

I call for the Happy dog, who it seems
has wisely slunk away somewhere,
and when she comes in I can see right off
she's swelled up fat as a full-blown tick.

So, worried she might up and croak,
I load her in the car and head for the country,
thinking a run might do her some good, and it does
I guess, 'cuz after a couple of miles and several
healthy deposits, she seems okay and we head back.
I open the car-door and she jumps in,
then onto the backseat just in time
to chuck up what remains of that chicken
on the floor of my Mercury.

After a robust round of cursing, and thanks
to gas-stop eateries for the napkins of various pedigrees
I find here and there in the car, I start cleaning,
'cuz I've had dogs enough to know if I don't
what's left of that chicken's gonna get recycled
and we can start the whole process over again.

So I get it done, and once again
load the Happy dog, who's shrunk some now,
almost back to her fit-and-trim self,
and a couple of proverbs come to mind—
All's Well That Ends Well,
and Happy Is As Happy Does.
But a whole damn chicken—Jesus!
It ain't like I don't feed her.
What the hell's she thinking?

February 1977

I was four months out of the army and bent
on drinking up my unemployment,
since mid-October through January
they hadn't found available work for me,
construction laborer cum infantryman.
Then it warmed up and they called me in,
said a crew putting up a new department-
store could use a block-layer's assistant.
So I signed on and proceeded to haul
the block and mud to that damned east wall.
By the end of the first day it was clear
how much that block-layer liked his beer.
Every hour or two required a trip to town.
I'm surprised the whole building ain't come down.

History Lesson

"Bonn's good," my brother said,
when I asked who he'd recommend
for History class in high school.
"Just make sure you don't *ever* piss him off."

Mr. Bonn was a solid 5-foot-8
and near 200 pounds,
a former Golden Gloves champ
and present regular down at The Mint.

He was warm as toast that first week,
just a little rosy about the cheeks
(possibly a case of razor burn),
but then a few students pushed the envelope.

One bright morning in the second week,
he entered with his usual stack of books,
then paused for a moment at the door
when the noise in the classroom just kept on.

He ambled over to his desk at the front
and slammed! those books down so damned hard
the whole room shook into silent terror,
two dozen wide-eyed students staring

at a face so suddenly livid it seemed
it might be the barrel-chested devil himself
beginning a lesson on impending doom
in an eerily quiet and measured voice.

Devolution

Dreaming is now the common fate,
human awareness under assault
from myriad channels of illusion,
hour to hour volleys of *new, improved*
products promising a better you,
shorter surgeries, longer-acting drugs,
a wealth of quick fixes already proven
to fragment being into episodes
of frenzied anxiety, then boredom. But
rest assured of a painless existence,
however shortened due to side effects,
your life wrapped in the great web, hanging
in the shadow of an economy
both bankrupt and booming,
business-as-usual politicians
proffering the impossible, each vying
for that vacant office—returned Christ,
while self-glorified zealots roar,
ignorantly seeking to devour
the few among us who still believe
in a god incarnate in us all.

Where the Waters
Take You

Where the Waters Take You

Again on that pilgrimage all must make,
even with others you walk alone
to the sacred pool grown clear and warm
through the ages in its cup of rock,
the spring where all waters originate,
in the underworld, the river of death
sweeping you out of the familiar myth,
down that fork into an alternate fate,
a warm subterranean stream
where, washed of all that you must forget,
everything formerly accepted as true,
you lose yourself once more and begin
the dark, difficult passage out
to wherever the waters take you.

If

If ever I look again
into those paradise eyes
and discover that mystic
flame still burning
the forbidden way back
to the forgotten tree,
I'll damn it all again and fall
blazing back to the Garden,
so hot this time
not even God
will put me out
alive.

Bone Story

Lost page of a forgotten epic
turned over to the reading of a river,
this scarred, now-petrified relic
rode floods through millennia to surface here,
a polished piece of shattered bone,
elemental to some previous chapter
in a drama now forever gone,
rendering a literal reading of scripture
a simple blasphemy. On these fresh dunes
the eternally-evolving Creation
opens to all who read the runes,
who trust the gift of imagination
to explain what no other faculty can,
theology too young to understand.

Gravity

—after Marjorie Saiser's "Each Wrong
Choice Was a Horse I Saddled"

Raised by our Lutheran mothers, we went
looking for rather than avoiding trouble,
the crazier, more dangerous the better,
moderation anathema—
drinking, fighting, always gambling,
betting tomorrow would never come,
rising mornings with little or no
memory of a night before.

Mad, wild, scared, always running,
we joined the army on a goddamn whim
and the perennial party was over.

The inevitable scars in time took you
to New Orleans and a graceful death,
while I go on drinking, gambling, having grown
too old to put up much of a fight,
though I still feel *the animal beneath me*,
and deeper, the Earth, this timeless Mother
for unknown reasons still engaged
in rocking me down to sleep.

—for Leon

Lambrecht Auto Sales, Pierce Nebraska

Well, the big Chevy sale's over now.
They say people came from all around,
even a few from overseas, to see
and bid on those classic autos,
some with only a handful of miles.

I'd heard about those cars for years,
and no doubt it was a memorable event,
but I don't care that much for crowds,
and anyway I've got reason enough
to remember Lambrecht Chevrolet.

My brother bought his first car there,
a dark blue '53 Ford 2-door,
flathead 8, 3-speed on the column,
assuring me that that sweet machine
would take us to the river anytime we wanted,
no more waiting around for Mom.

And it did, for a time, before taking
my brother and his newly-found, need-a-ride friends
off to the drive-in, pool hall, parties,
me left facing two years alone
before I could get some wheels of my own.

Daybreak on the Dismal

Friday afternoon, Memorial weekend,
eight men pile their tents and supplies
into a pair of vans and head west
towing a trailer with four canoes.

A couple of hundred miles later,
camped beside a Sandhills river,
they start a fire after dinner
and lighten their coolers long into the night.

A pre-dawn cloud of dense fog
dampening all but the sound of water,
one man on a roadside table wakes
under a blanket wet with dew.

Groaning, he sits up, pulls on shoes,
jogs a mile and back on the highway,
the infantry's go-to method
for resurrecting its dead-drunks.

As the sun climbs the eastern hills,
a distant cow bawls upstream,
and he lifts a breakfast bottle in salute—
daybreak on the Dismal.

The Other River

High, hidden, flowing only at night
from the sacred source watering the world,
I've glimpsed it a mere handful of times,
always at dusk, always alone.
The surface from a distance seems serene,
but nearer you feel an unfathomed force
and know that a careless approach
would end with you suddenly swept away.

Still, there are those who would attempt
to dam it to harness that power,
but ignorant of such otherness,
they will never discover this river,
for the waters of life, high, hidden,
flow only by night, and forever.

Dominion

—after a photograph by Gary Entsminger
and a poem by David Lee

—Genesis 1:28, John 19:11

Studying the Point in the photograph,
the barren top of the mesa
and that sheer drop some thousand feet
to the Colorado River,

a poem and its epigraph come to mind,
stark images, harsh echoes,
that wild herd of fenced-in ghosts
still haunting Dead Horse Point.

What sacrilegious words men plied
in their ancient manufacture of a god
who would grant them full dominion,
condoning such brazen subterfuge—

wedding stolen goods to goodness,
veiling power in ritual religion,
greed white-washed in a gown of law,
bridal camouflage for the gross
and godless lusts of humankind.

She Quilts Her Dreams

The abandoned farmstead haunts her dreams,
and she quilts it in her waking hours—
one block of cloth for the empty cupboards,
one for the cracked boots on the porch,

one for the traps full of old mouse bones,
another for the rusted pump in the yard,
one for the garden fence falling down
around her choked and dying flowers,

one block for the fields long gone to weeds,
another for the barn with the hanging doors,
one for the ghost of the mare in her stall,
and marring the milk-white center block

one bold stitching the color of blood
or a spent shot-shell in the snow.

Haiku Masters

Feather-light, their words
descend on the sleeping heart
with piercing talons.

Remembrance

Preparing antelope steak and eggs
for breakfast, once again I remember
how, when and where this animal died—
a thirty-caliber bullet
on a warm October morning
in broken grassland on the panhandle.
I will not forget the sudden end
of a life lived in that wild place.

What I'm cooking is no simple meal,
nor am I callous to this creature's demise.
I'd fully regret that morning if I could
imagine a quicker, more meaningful death.
But in the barren badland breaks where she died
there is naturally no such option.

The Borderland

What in your life is calling you
when all the noise is silenced
—Rumi

Up in the panhandle, headed northwest,
at some point you cross an imaginary line
and all at once you're in South Dakota,
or if you've angled more to the west, Wyoming.
Either way you're alone in a wild country,
high plains sagebrush, cactus, yucca,
a vast open space with no meaningful limit,
and you may be lost, yet it seems familiar,
no more than a fleeting dream perhaps,
but you feel you've seen all this before.

And your entire concept of time wavers
as you question how you know this place.
Were you predator here, then, or prey—
cautiously stalking your next meal
across this broken dreamscape
seeded with prehistoric bone,
or racing, lungs a frantic bellows
fueling another sprint across this land
where flight is the lone redeemer?

Eventually your attention returns
from that timeless space to the present,
and noting the level of your remaining fuel
you turn onto a fork that trails southeast,
supposed direction of the illusive border,
where you follow faint ruts that become a road
out to a highway that tells you you're back
in northwest Nebraska, though by now you know
you never leave the borderland.

To the TransCanada Pipe-liners
Attempting to Re-Map Nebraska

To certify where the Sandhills start,
take a drive down one of those section lines
west of Pierce in an old low-rider,
like the one my brother years ago
thought a primo grouse-hunting vehicle,
loud, dual glass-packs baling-wired
to the cross-member supporting that massive
three-speed tranny in his '58 Ford,
cool modifications hanging so low they
soon high-centered the whole damned works
on the ridge of sand between the ruts.

But like my brother, don't let up
when your rig stops going anywhere but down,
just keep cursing and goosing the gas
till you're in so deep there's nothing left
but a two-mile jaunt to the nearest place
with a tractor to haul your tough ass out.

Repeat this process a time or three,
and revise your map accordingly.

Valkyrie

That July, my brother found his ten-year-old
Labrador/husky cross dead on the road.

When I asked about his dog the following day,
he told me where he'd buried
the closest companion he'd had from the time
Ares had been a pocket-size pup.

That November, hunting together,
I saw my brother smile and give a subtle wave
at every hawk hovering above,
perched on a post or in some dead tree.

And in time I saw that summer morning,
him walking out to his dog on the road,
and nearby, a hawk rising as though
having waited for him through the night.

Transfiguration

Yesterday it was hard to swallow
those old tales of daylight growing
dim under flocks of migrating birds.
But today a cloud of starlings
pouring south over Beaver Creek
affords plenty of time to wonder
who first imagined them the progeny
of those far-off lights in the heavens.

Bearing a night sky in miniature
on each of their innumerable bodies,
they amass under a common spirit
until no individual remains,
just miles of darkness overhead,
the sky-wide shadow of a living god.

Even Here, Even Now

A far train sounds
long blasts to the south

as I open the curtain
on another winter day,

sun all but lost in the gray sky
hanging over last night's snow.

I turn up the thermostat,
start the coffee.

The furnace cycles on,
stirs the chimes above the stove,

five thin brass tubes
beneath a miniature pagoda

joined all at once
in wordless prayer,

in Nebraska,
in December,

half a world west of the Orient
and on a windless morning.

Silence

The annual symphony winds down,
the instrumentalist sections done,

the bees, birds, bullfrogs of spring,
the sawing cicadas of summer,

even the autumn woodwinds,
stripped of their last crisp reeds,

now, at last, the music of snow—
(crescendo)

A Walk in the Morning,
A Walk at the End of Day

This morning before the rain began,
an oblivious woman in earphones
came down the sidewalk across the street,
bringing to mind my mother and her friend,
their ritual walk around the block,
before Rachel moved out to the Meadows,
where she died a few weeks before Mom.

After months of drought, this September rain
left a pool at the bottom of the drive,
where a dove now descends from the grace of flight
and waddles down toward the water,
moving against the awkward pull of earth
as that increasingly alien weight,
the body, bears down at the end of day.

To Come of Decent Age

When I'm no longer young
let me be able to make wine
from chokecherries and care enough
to let it age.

—Stephen Dunn
"The Carpenter's Song"

Another stanza in that epic
document of life and love, at last
discovering the value inherent
in a craft handed down through generations—
picking wild fruit, fermenting the must,
then waiting for it to come of decent age,
a patient process, in every way
similar to the long, slow maturation
of a boy who once found a dozen bottles
shelved in his grandparents' basement,
uncorked one and helped himself
to a first taste of rhubarb wine,
and fifty years later raised a glass
of chokecherry he'd made on his own.

No Wine, No Wafer

I'm cold-smoking brine-cured venison,
temp in the forties, snow on the ground,
something like revising a rough first draft,
this long, slow process of making meat.

There is an art to it, after all,
though many consider it simply craft—
a hunt, a kill, gutting, butchering,
coarse words now that once were common.

But then there's brining, smoking, sausage-making,
and taking the time to do it right,
honoring an animal that gave its life,
no virtual-sacrament wine and wafer,
but a once-living flesh-and-blood sacrifice.

This beautiful creature died for me,
as others have died for many of you.
But hunting allows no ignorant denial.
Each autumn, the warmth that stains my hands
is the literal blood of an actual Christ.

The Air We Breathe

Most noticeable when it begins to move
otherwise stationary objects,
the leaves in the oak by the alley,
chimes on the corner of the garage,
small naked branches in the neighborhood trees,
upright grasses, overhead wires,
those intangible shadows cast by the above
drifting first one direction, then another.

This atmosphere that envelopes it all,
originating who can say where,
renders it rather inane to question
the existence of a spiritual realm
while inhaling an essence that animates
each of us wholly as a ghost.

Photochemistry

Just after dawn this January morning
I open the kitchen shades and find
an odd flocking on the east window,
small frost chevrons, some with tails,
suspended over the lower sash,
each a distinct individual,
dozens of them clouding the glass
and the neighborhood trees beyond,
resembling a mass of waterfowl,
far white geese in a photograph
nearly developed but not yet fixed,
the image, too soon exposed to the sun,
already beginning that slow-motion fade
out of its frame on the wall.

Even in Winter

This morning everything's wrapped in ice,
aglaze with yesterday's gentle rain
after the temperature drop last night,
a skin of hard water sealing the street,
clear glass sheeting vehicles, power lines,
the diamond patterns in the chain-link fence,
those ornamental trees across the alley
suddenly adorned with leaves of light,
naked branches sparkling here and there
with colors of the visible spectrum
most apparent after summer storms,
but decorating a January morning
with this similarly striking work
by those gods of life, the sun and rain.

Slivers of Light

For man has closed himself up, till he sees
all things thro' narrow chinks of his cavern.
—William Blake

Slow and silent, the progression of Orion
through a map of frost at the window.

That instant Earth's tilt reverses at solstice,
déjà vu in a foreign land.

Far-off, the trilling of invisible cranes,
a fairy ring of mushrooms on the lawn.

Sudden mass resurrection of cicadas,
a maze of beaver-work along the creek.

The companionate scents of hay and horses,
crickets heralding the night.

A coyote pup lost in prayer to the moon,
colored dogs circling the sun.

The natural world in all her seasons,
awareness scratching at the door.

Chicken-Oodle!

—for Roger

Now you and that soup stop are both long gone,
but whenever I near Thedford I remember.
Just out of the army, I was no volunteer, but when you asked,
with a simple shrug I became part of your crew,

loading a pair of vans with necessities for the annual
float trip down the Dismal—half-a-dozen large coolers,
each one packed full of ice and someone's favorite brew,
a bottle or two of cheap wine, Mellow Days or Easy Nights,

a meager nod toward edibles, that wilderness staple, hot dogs,
some packaged Polish sausages, bacon and a few dozen eggs,
a cardboard box containing utensils, buns, and bags of chips.
one van towing a trailer with our four canoes and river gear.

Eight of us heading west, back in the '70s,
cassette players un-*realing* the miles to "Luckenbach Texas,"
"Okie from Muskogee," "Up Against the Wall,
Redneck Mother," each tune carrying our caravan closer

to that gas station east of Thedford, where once more
you'd holler into the C.B. mic, *Chicken-Oodle! Don't forget!*
reminding us again of that sacred shrine,
the gas-stop coin-op soup machine,

where one truly memorable Memorial weekend, that salty
steaming liquid saved us after two long days and nights of rain,
tents and sleeping bags soaked clean through, temps somewhere
low down in the forties, our wet hands gone numb on the paddles,

sodden butts stuck to aluminum seats, some thoughtful soul's
precious pint of brandy all-too-soon sucked way-too-dry,
nothing but icy beers for solace as we paddled, waded
and towed our canoes out to the Highway 83 bridge, and

the frigid ordeal over at last, we gathered at the gas-stop east of town,
where you discovered that soup machine, and every year after
brought it back to mind. And like an echo, still, when I near Thedford—
Chicken-Oodle! Don't forget!

The Long Act of Falling

In a cotton shirt and cutoff jeans,
socks rolled over his boot-tops,
he crosses the New Fork on a fallen pine,
one of dozens spanning the river
at the crossing a mile and a half below
that steep descent on the Palmer Lake trail,
the long way down from Cutthroat Lakes.

Half-way across another of those trees
I stopped and snapped the photograph
I keep on the wall above my desk,
an eleven-by-fourteen black-and-white,
the best of those I shot back then,
an un-posed study of a friend, now dead,
crossing his last wild river.

Under the sun or the camera's magic
he appears outlined in fine bright light:
white hair, chin, the top of his pack,
shirt-front, forearm, hands, one thigh
ablaze in a silver, ghost-thin aura
as he leans forward, staring down
at the log ahead of his left foot,
fully considering his next step
atop that round and rotting bridge,

as if his life depends on it,
as though he sees the steps to come,
the diagnosis of the specialist,
surgery, a metal valve in a heart
long scarred from rheumatic fever,
then blood thinner, regular checkups and
the end of trekking into wilderness.

Beyond and above him, in its narrow cut,
the river runs black in a white-rock bed,
skirting boulders the size of old bulls
in its rush down that horizontal ladder of trees
toppled from the canyon walls where
three tall pines lean over the water
in the long act of falling.

In an Otherwise Empty Sky

In response to something like instinct
the first word rises, others follow,

and a new migration begins
the archetypal bid for survival,

direction perhaps predetermined
back at the beginning of time,

soon lines of words almost seem to fly
like birds in an otherwise empty sky.

The Evening Watch

Each spring melting snows and rains
wash layers of bone from the yellow clay
at the foot of these naked river bluffs,
where down through the ages bison died.

As the day winds down, in the fading light
the view of that broken ridge brings to mind
a painting of a man at prayer, long ago,
three friends fast asleep nearby.

Alone in this wild place at dusk,
hearing again that haunting question
when he turns to wake his friends,
I close my eyes, begin to see.

And from the river bluffs to the horizon and on
the stacked bones watch with me.

ACKNOWLEDGMENTS

Grateful acknowledgment to the editors of the publications in which
these poems previously appeared:

Nebraska Life
   "This Bike Path Now Called the Cowboy Trail"
   "Spring Burial in the Sandhills"
   "Ode to an Outhouse"
Paddlefish
   "Lawn Care with Babe"
Pinyon Review
   "A Walk Along the River"
   "The Jungle"
   "Already There"
   "Uncle Don"
   "Dominion"
Haiku Journal
   "Haiku Masters"
Nebraska Poetry: A Sesquicentennial Anthology, 1867-2017
   "This Bike Path Now Called the Cowboy Trail"
   "Spring Burial in the Sandhills"
2018 Magic Oxygen Literary Prize Anthology
   "Transfiguration"
Back in the Animal Kingdom
   "The Long Act of Falling"

My thanks to all those who saw many of these poems as they developed
and offered their thoughtful insights: Barbara Schmitz, Bonnie Johnson
Bartee, Diane Blinn, Grizz McIntosh, Jim Reese, JV Brummels, Karen
Wingett, Lin Brummels, Lisa Sandlin, Maureen Kingston, Scott Abels,
and Tana Buoy.

And special thanks to Gary and Susan Entsminger at Pinyon Publishing
for your always meaningful suggestions.

CPSIA information can be obtained
at www.ICGtesting.com
Printed in the USA
LVHW090326111218
600013LV00001B/9/P

9 781936 671502